32/100

Stop Flocking Around

What Alex the Albatross Can Teach You About Navigating Change

Soaring together

Written by Karen Collacutt & Karen Kessler

Illustrations by Carmen Van Essen

 FriesenPress

One Printers Way
Altona, MB R0G 0B0
Canada

www.friesenpress.com

ISBN
978-1-03-910178-4 (Hardcover)
978-1-03-910177-7 (Paperback)
978-1-03-910179-1 (eBook)

Self-Help, Personal Growth

Distributed to the trade by The Ingram Book Company

We dedicate this book to
the seeker in each of us

Table of Contents

Foreword: Alex the Albatross Changed

So far, life checks all the boxes. Alex is warm in this small world. There is a familiar voice chirping in the background, and a never-ending food supply. The only fuss is when the egg flips over, or the light changes quickly and disturbs the deepest of slumber.

Things settle into a rhythm that is familiar and safe. Even when there is a surprise flip, there is trust that everything will settle soon enough . . . and it does. Until one day, it doesn't.

The signs are subtle at first. The egg starts to get cramped. Then the noise and bustle outside ramp up. All this just after the food runs out. The need to peck the shell starts automatically as a new sensation of hunger awakens in Alex's body. The egg suddenly seems extraordinarily small.

Time seems to stand still amid all the effort and focus. Then, for the first time, air rushes into this world. Alex is upside down. Tired from pecking and just wanting some help, Alex is unaware how vital it is to claim this new world. As the new world floods in, the senses feel assaulted—it is louder, brighter, and so confusing. Alex leans heavily on instinct, and in that moment breaks free.

Looking around, Alex notices others who are also tired and cranky. There are a few other naked birds squawking for food and huddling for warmth. As the next day dawns, Alex understands this about the world: sometimes it's bright, then it's dark, and the straw of the nest is always pokey. Over a few cycles, a routine starts to appear. Big birds bring food and cover everyone for warmth and protection. Alex wonders what else this new world has in store.

Days pile up and restlessness grows as fast as feathers. Sometimes the wind catches a wing while they are playing and one of them lifts up a bit. So scary and fun! Everyone talks about flying out of their nest and taking to the skies. But it's all just talk. Every one of them is still there waiting when the big birds come back with supper.

Decision Day doesn't start any differently for Alex. There isn't any clue that this will be such an important day. All the playing in the surf and wind has only been fun and games until now. Alex catches sight of other young albatross running awkwardly toward the water, taking a great leap, getting some air, and then landing in the water. Alex watches as the other birds march back up the beach again and again. It is quite a sight and Alex laughs at how focused these young albatross are, seemingly unaware of the spectacle . . . until one of them catches air and begins to climb higher . . . and higher. The wind brings back the cry of joy to their ears.

In that instant, Alex sets sights on the skies too.

All day Alex wears a track back to the start of the runway, learning all the ways to not get into the air. It is tiring and still Alex perseveres.

Then, with a mix of will, updraft, and timing, Alex is airborne. The emotions coursing through this albatross's body are mixed and intense. The option to land right away flickers through Alex's thoughts and is immediately abandoned—flying high is the goal and it is time to enjoy it.

Over the following weeks Alex spends time landing, taking off, learning to fish, and creating ease in flight. New skills present themselves to hone and the new strength building in Alex's muscles proves up for the task. By the end of the season, Alex leaves the little island, traveling thousands of leagues, soaring gracefully, and reveling in the joy of flight.

It is all worth it.

The Change Journey

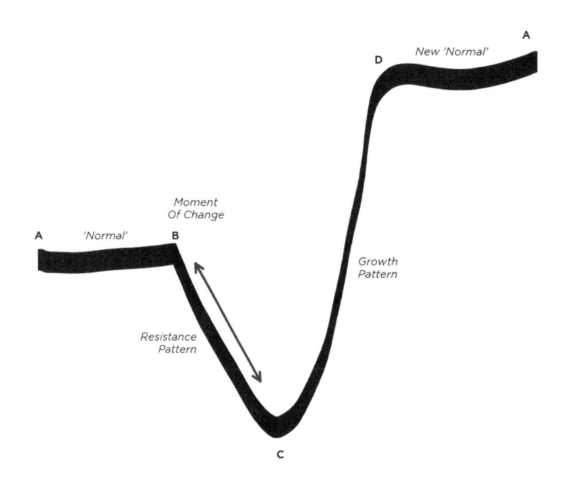

The Change Journey

Change happens. It feels crazy, like there is no rhyme or reason to it. We are ticking along in our normal life and, by choice or by circumstance, suddenly everything is different.

That's change and it happens all the time, to all of us. Sometimes the changes are tiny and fast. Sometimes they are huge and can take a week, a month, a year, or a lifetime. One thing we know is that we all have multiple changes going on at once—all in different stages.

What if we told you that there is a process for change? An actual map that you can use to orient yourself and predict the next steps?

Imagine the change process like a journey. There are landmarks, updrafts, and crosswinds along the way. We also have our own internal compass to guide us. All helpful . . . if you have a map.

Whew! Do you feel better already?

Without the map, the landmarks and updrafts and crosswinds just look like part of the chaotic landscape, and our internal compass seems to wing around in circles. When we know there is a map and can identify where we are on it, the landmarks and updrafts begin to make sense. We can expect the crosswinds and fly straight into them.

First Things First: An Introduction

Car Brilliance

New revelations and "Aha"s are common in our circle. We love to fly high and move forward our understanding of how the world works. You might even say we have a bit of an addiction. We love the energy that comes from expanding our understanding of how our amazing human experience works in this world.

March 27th, 2019 will go down in the books as one such evening for us. We attended Dionne Thomson and Leanne Quesnelle's Wise Women Say event in Midland, Ontario, Canada. Karen Collacutt was speaking. Karen Kessler saw the glimmer of new possibilities around an older topic—the human experience and resistance to change. She became quite animated with her growing excitement (there were sketches and everything!).

On the way home, the magic bubbled and we dubbed it "Car Brilliance," recording the whole thing. The depth of the conversation revealed the challenges of change and the true nature of "stuck." Once we got that, we knew what to do about it.

We've Been There

We have lived the struggle through change our whole lives. We have watched ourselves, our friends, colleagues, and family members spin as they try to find steady footing through change.

Struggling to Take Flight

We saw that every person was willing to do the work. Every person was resilient enough to make the journey, provided they were always moving forward. But sometimes, they just couldn't tell which way was up, let alone forward! They needed a map.

As leaders, Neuro-Linguistic Programming trainers, and Master Coaches, we knew we had the tools, and there was still confusion about why some clients and colleagues moved through the journey more quickly than others. And most frustratingly, we questioned why some decided to quit when we could see how close they were!

We knew that this inspiration would not come as clearly again. This inspiration was for us to action together and share widely. This was a book. So, still in the car, still blown away, we committed fully to this project. You might ask, what did "commit fully" mean?

We knew we needed to commit to immediate action and plan even more action. (And then more action.)

We knew what would happen—resistance, nervousness, testing of our commitment. (Crap!) All of this would happen before the small successes that would build the momentum to carry our project through. We were going to be the test subjects and lab technicians all at once.

Our journey has been interesting to say the least, from cleaning coffee off the ceiling and walking circles around buildings, to some general freaking out. We engaged with our top peeps to cheer for us as we took action and sat in awe as our focus groups validated our messages for you over and over again.

We have learned so much about how change works and the dance between being stuck and having momentum. As we wrote, learned, validated, wrote, grew, validated, and wrote, we fell more and more in love with you, our readers. You very real people who, like us, change again and again.

For those of you who are ready to
- create space for miracles in your world,
- dial down the self-induced stress,
- master the Change Journey, and
- be curious about what the world has in store,

we have unlocked the secrets of change for you.

Flying high,

Karen and Karen

Why We Chose the Albatross

When we learned that the largest flying bird on the planet has a wingspan up to 4 metres (13 feet), is incredibly awkward getting into the air, and then dynamically soars for thousands of leagues without needing to land, we realized that it sounds just like us!

Karen and I started by searching YouTube for videos of albatross learning to take off. The awkward sway, attempting to hold those wings aloft, while running across the sand was inspiring and fun to watch. The wind would catch one wing and they would be off track. Their tenacity was so strong you could only root for them as you started to want the sky as much as they did.

We read about "dynamic soaring" and were amazed as we dove into the research. Imagine creating your own speed and altitude without flapping your wings. To know that it is possible to travel great distances by being in tune with your environment, by leveraging what is happening around you instead of forcing your way through the gale

As we compared the albatross's journey to the skies and our own human journey, we found that it was the perfect metaphor.

1. Hang out with family and enjoy life

2. Play with the idea of change

3. Practise and play—but not really go anywhere

4. Make the decision to fly

5. Feel awkward and silly at the beginning

6. Build the muscle and skill

7. Gracefully soar and see the world

How to Use This Book

You are likely going through some change in your world. Yeah! And we are sorry. Sometimes change shows up as steady winds, like Alex's, and more often as stormy weather. In fact, it normally shows up with a weather alert.

Alex isn't the only one on a journey—we have created this journey for you.

We offer this book as a lesson, a tool, and a resource to read front to back the first time and then revisit as needed through the changes in your world. The Change Journey is a predictable process that, with practise, you can navigate more and more gracefully.

Part One: Because You Are Important

We invite you to imagine what's possible, claim your amazing self, and choose to be open. Use this part to expand your perspectives for a smoother path through change.

Part Two: The Journey Begins Here

Did you love Alex's successful Change Journey? In this Part we dive into how the Change Journey shows up in your world. The good, the bad, and the ugly of it. When you know what the journey looks like, you can tell where you are and whether you are pointed in the right direction.

Part Three: Master Change

Once you are ready to smooth out the edges, shorten the trip, and migrate confidently through your change, then it is time for tools. This part has the essential tools. Join us online for many more at www.alexthealbatross.com.

Part One: Because You Are Important

Audacity to Imagine a Fabulous Future

Change can seem like a long winding abyss—forever "working on it." It might feel like you are measuring your world by the daily amount of suck or hope.

We are here to tell you that whether you made a bold choice or are being tested by a changing world, it is time to find your footing, release the past, and have the audacity to dream. Navigating this change is more than possible—it's a journey with identifiable landmarks and a repeatable process.

The journey requires your audacity.

Audacity is the willingness to see a new future—a future where you are more than you have ever been before. It is allowing the flame of inspiration to ignite within you, light you up from inside. You shine. Audacity continues to bloom.

When you have audacity, you take steps forward. You believe in possibilities. You set yourself up for success and pull on the resources that will support you—like this book!

I know—it feels like a big deal to step into this new future. It is easy to start to second-guess yourself, especially when others can't see how it all might turn out.

Here is what you need to know—you have already started changing.

Your job at this point is to lean in—to have the audacity to imagine a fabulous future. It feels big and it is. Yeah!

Be audacious. Act. Keep reading.

A Case for Worthiness

If you don't believe you are worthy of your audacious future, nothing we can say will change that. We are not going to attempt to convince you. Instead, we invite you to be curious—what if you ARE worthy of all the possibilities?

When you believe you are worthy or are curious about what happens when you embrace the truth of your worthiness, several things open up for you on your journey.

- **Like Attracts Like:** When you choose to believe in your worthiness, you are open to feeling love and belonging. You attract more love and belonging, and willingly accept it as it arrives. This keeps you in a recharge cycle that accelerates your change.
- **Noticing Opportunities:** There is a part of your brain in charge of pointing out opportunities that match your beliefs. When you believe in your worthiness, you notice the opportunities that go with it.
- **Deeper Beliefs:** Every experience serves to reinforce your belief that you are worthy of the audacious dream you have envisioned. Emotions build and your actions deepen your belief and the inherent benefits.

What do you do if you have yet to realize you are worthy? Earn it. We are serious. Take the actions that someone who is worthy would take. This is one of those times where "fake it till you make it" actually works.

As you progress, you will feel good about your efforts and start to realize the initial glimmerings of worthiness. It will build, and by the time you achieve your audacious future, you will be proud to call it your own.

Model of the World

You have a unique perspective called your Model of the World. It's your little slice of truth, your viewpoint.

Your Model of the World is created by your life experiences, beliefs, and attitudes, what you were taught, and what you value. It creates a filter through which you experience and assign meaning to your world. This is how two people can have such different experiences in the same situation.

When you receive new information, you filter it through your Model of the World and decide what it means for you.

Your Model of the World is designed to evolve over time. Some people hold onto their Model of the World so tightly, getting more and more invested, that they become unwilling to see any other perspective. Once they are resistant to new ideas, change feels hard and they get grumpy.

Alternatively, you can choose to be open, be curious, and anticipate new perspectives. This allows you to be much more flexible and graceful through the Change Journey.

We wonder what new perspectives are in store for you.

Hmmm. It's good to wonder.

Part Two: The Journey Begins Here

Alex's story is relevant for all of us. Let's dive in.

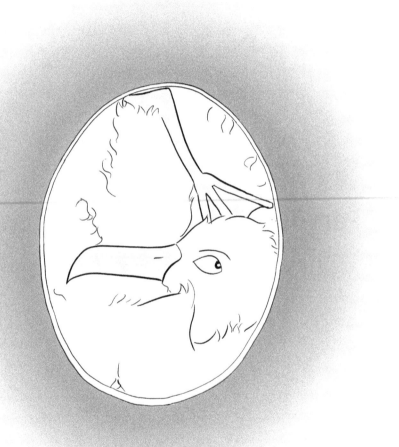

Section One: The Egg

Comfy world comes undone.

Life in Your Five-Star Egg

So far, life checks all the boxes. Alex is warm in the egg. There is a familiar voice chirping in the background, and a never-ending food supply. The only fuss is when the egg flips over, or the light changes quickly and disturbs the deepest of slumber.

We go to great lengths to create our "Normal." Protecting it becomes a full-time affair and includes our work, our family, our hobbies, and our daily routines.

Whether our "normal" is warm, safe, and well fed, or chaotic and tiring, we have knowledge and mastery of every inch of our world. We are quickly annoyed when external forces turn our world upside down and infringe on our plans.

It makes complete sense. Even if we are people who like change, we want to do it on our own terms. We expect others to meet us where we are so that we can reduce conflict and needless stress. Great effort is placed on creating a world we can depend on day in and day out.

When the whole day goes our way, we feel confident and wear a big smile. We are thinking *I totally nailed it, I have arrived!* or some form of *I have finally got this life thing figured out—now I can relax.*

We all know what happens next.

Cracks in the Egg

The signs are subtle at first. The egg starts to get cramped. Then the noise and bustle outside ramp up. All of this just after the food runs out. The need to peck the shell starts automatically as a new sensation of hunger awakens in Alex's body. The egg suddenly seems extraordinarily small.

Such a human thing to do. We finally get everything the way we want it, and then start pecking it apart. The act of creating our "normal" develops skills, connects us with resources, and changes how we interact with our world. We grow—often more than we ever imagine.

Growth is a continual thing and soon we outgrow the very thing we spent days, months, or years dreaming, hoping, and wishing for. D'oh!

Dissatisfaction sets in. We are growing and our environment is just not keeping up. Our Model of the World plays a key role in how we explain our dissatisfaction to ourselves and others. Although infinite, here are some of our favourites:

- I should feel more gratitude for what I have—others aren't as lucky
- If they would just get their act together everything would be perfect
- I am not keeping up my end so I can't expect them to keep up theirs
- I need more self-care—I am just stressed because I don't meditate enough
- Things are not working out because I just haven't been putting in the effort

The thing is that, deep down, we have been moving forward the whole time. No matter how we have been explaining the signs away, change is about to be delivered to our door.

And Then One Day . . .

New air rushes into this world. Alex is upside down. Tired from pecking and just wanting some help, Alex is unaware how vital it is to claim this new world. As the new world floods in, the senses feel assaulted—it is louder, brighter, and so confusing. Alex leans heavily on instinct, and in that moment breaks free.

Confusion comes with big shifts. Our old Model of the World, now in pieces, swirls chaotically around us. It is evolving, and our Model of the World slowly rebuilds around us—with holes. The holes are designed for us to plug in new knowledge, new resources, new skills, and other fun things.

The challenge is that no one ever tells us *how* to change. We misdiagnose what is happening and decide that we are wrong or broken. This results in:

- blame, grief, and emotional overload,
- fear and panic, or
- fight or flight response.

We end up questioning our choices, the people around us, and sometimes our own fitness for adulthood. Our focus becomes getting back to dry land—making everything the way it was.

The good news is that our life, in these moments, has turned into pure potential. We are invited to use this energy to create the next chapter of our story. Awareness of the gift of the chaos allows us to act decisively. We can take years off the journey ahead.

The moment we choose to lean into our instincts, we break free.

Section Two: Life in the Nest

Yeah! (And we are sorry.)

Chaos of the Nest

Turns out you are not the only one tired and cranky. There are a few other naked birds squawking for food and huddling for warmth. As the next day dawns, Alex understands this about the world: sometimes it's bright, then it's dark, and the straw of the nest is always pokey. Over a few cycles, a routine starts to appear. Big birds bring food and cover everyone for warmth and protection.

Whether we decided we wanted something different in our world or the carpet was unceremoniously pulled out from underneath our feet, the experience is the same for us all.

There is a sudden disorientation. If we look closely, even the familiar seems off.

Our response to this moment in the Change Journey will depend greatly on how many times we have traveled this pattern, and how aware we are of our place in the journey. It will be a variation of one (or more) of the following:

- **White hot anger:** Searching for who to blame and punish, sword held high.
- **Consigned:** Lost and sitting in the dirt waiting for someone to come and save us.
- **Confused and searching:** Looking for a sign or someone to point the way.
- **"D'oh!":** A sneaking suspicion that the wine-induced rant of truth from last Saturday was an invocation that has come to pass.
- **Oh, hello!:** Recalling this pattern and the need to keep moving forward no matter what.
- **Way ahead of you:** Wings are out, and we have totally got this!

Aware of it or not, this is not the first time we have walked this path. Nor will it be the last. Weary from walking? Choose to fly!

Playing in the Nest

Days pile up and restlessness grows as fast as feathers. Sometimes the wind catches a wing while they are playing and one of them lifts up a bit. So scary and fun! Everyone talks about flying out of their nests and taking to the skies. But it's all just talk. Every one of them is still there waiting when the big birds come back with supper.

There is a tension inherent in the change cycle. The pressure builds around us, purposefully, until it reaches into our awareness. At this moment of awareness, we are at a choice point. Do we:

a. use the energy from all the chaos, uncertainty, and frustration to move us forward into the unknown—effectively yielding to what we are creating, or

b. focus on how we can take the pressure off, and feel more comfortable in the moment?

Hear this—it is so normal to just be focused on releasing the pressure. Finding that sense of clarity, confidence, and clairvoyance that came from the old normal we had mastered. We even feel a longing for that about which we used to complain.

What we can promise is that the pressure will continue to build, and build, and build. The choice point will be presented to us again and again. It starts as a whisper, then a nudge, then a shout. We have free will and the choice will always be there for us—we have never missed it.

May "feeling stuck" be our clue that it is time to revisit the choice again—lean into the magnificent future each of us is creating, or cling to the illusion of safety in the nest for another round.

See you in the skies!

Standing on the Beach

Alex catches sight of other young albatross running awkwardly toward the water, taking a great leap, getting some air, and then landing in the water. Alex watches as the other birds march back up the beach again and again. It is quite a sight and Alex laughs at how focused these young albatross are, seemingly unaware of the spectacle . . .

Leaning in to embrace change can stir up old procrastination patterns. You might recognize some of your favourites:

- **The Dog Ate My Homework**: Finding excuses so you won't have to feel silly. This one can go on forever. Over time, it is possible to begin to believe your excuses more than you believe in yourself.

- **The Cheerleader**: Watching others instead of going for it. The sidelines can feel more comfortable, for sure, but will not satisfy.

- **The Academic**: Choosing to study so you don't have to "action." The funny thing is that you already know everything you need to begin. Action creates space for more knowledge to be incorporated. Just do it!

- **The Almost Ready**: Ready is not an emotion. You will never feel ready. So, instead, you might as well just jump in and go for it.

So, how about we just decide that all the head games in the world are just that—head games. They will never take you closer to the confident and competent version of you waiting on the other end of this journey.

Strap on those wings and look forward to surprising yourself. It can be fun to be silly and a lot more fun than just standing on the beach wishing you could fly.

Your Courage to Soar

. . . until one of them catches air and begins to climb higher . . . and higher. The wind brings back the cry of joy to their ears. In that instant, Alex sets sights on the skies too.

Ever wonder how people gather the courage to do the amazing things that they do? The truth is that the courage is only required to decide. Once the decision is well and truly made, courage is no longer a factor.

Woah, you say—how is that possible? Standing on the beach, our hearts are in our throats at the very thought of taking off!

Let's walk through this. First, the **formula for courage**: The amount of courage required is equal to the size of the gap between *who you believe you are* in this moment and *who you believe you need to be* to succeed. Since neither of these things are real, your estimation of the gap isn't real either.

Are you seeing the pattern? Courage is about what is in your head instead of what is real.

Three things are required to run this formula:

1. An illusion about *how* we believe we will do at something we have never done
2. An illusion about *who* we believe we need to be to do that thing we have never done
3. A focus on the *future* instead of our now

Every person who succeeds has decided to "action." The trick is to be curious about just how much smaller the gap is than it currently appears from this perspective. Let's go find out!

Section Three: Takeoff

You have decided—now what?

The Awkward Ascent

All day Alex wears a track back to the start of the runway, learning all the ways to not get into the air. It is tiring and still Alex perseveres.

Have you ever encouraged a little one to become a toddler? We celebrate the rolling over, then the crawling. We celebrate the pulling up to standing in the crib or by the coffee table. We celebrate the bouncing, then the first steps with their grasped fingers in our own as we walk behind. We celebrate their first two steps even after they land on their bum.

If we never suggest that a baby give up trying to walk after a few tries, why do so many adults give up on learning new skills when something goes wrong? There are four stages to building competence, and no matter our age, the steps are essential.

The **Four Stages of Competence** are:

1. **How could that be?** This is where we don't know just how much we don't know. When we watch others, new skills seem simple and straightforward.

2. **Oh!** This is the wake-up call. We realize that we don't know where to start, why things are working, and why we are so awkward.

3. **Nailed it!** We do better and better. When we focus and pay attention, we can nail it. When it doesn't go quite right, we can see the moment things went sideways. We learn from our missteps and can correct on the fly.

4. **That was easy**. Over time we master skills and truly own them. Others see us and think that seems simple and straightforward!

Lean into the expectations for the journey. Choose to embrace the fun and celebrate each growth marker—even when we land on our bums.

Reaching Altitude

Then, with a mix of will, updraft, and timing, Alex is airborne. The emotions coursing through this albatross's body are mixed and intense. The option to land right away flickers through Alex's thoughts and is immediately abandoned—flying high is the goal and it is time to enjoy it.

This step on our journey is filled with intense emotions. One of them is exhilaration, generally followed by some internal response. The attitudes of others and our previous experiences will dictate what internal response happens inside us just after the exhilaration floods our system.

- **Bail**: We spend all that time building up enough courage to decide. Then, as our bodies prepare for launch and that exhilaration moves through us, we misinterpret our experience as unsafe. In that moment we find an excuse and bail.

- **Lose Focus:** We experience the exhilaration and then get all up in our head about what we are feeling, our reasons for doing this, and what others think. This diminishes our sense of accomplishment. We lose momentum to stick with the change.

- **Nervous Laugh:** When it has been a long time since we stayed in any intense experience to the end, it can be a lot for our bodies to process. The nervous laugh or huge yawn is designed to process the excess energy. Do whatever you need to stay on track—the story and momentum will be worth it!

- **Ride the Dragon:** Exhilaration keeps flooding our system during the times we yield fully to the experience. It is an intoxicating experience. It marks us forever and fuels our journey.

Regardless of how we have handled this step in the past, we get to decide how we approach it now. It is time to choose.

Creating Your Own Flight Path

Over the following weeks, Alex spends time landing, taking off, learning to fish, and creating ease in flight. New skills present themselves to hone and the new strength building in Alex's muscles proves up for the task.

What we really need to master as we engage with change is *Dynamic Soaring*. It will assist with the change journey and get us back to enjoying our amazing lives. The albatross uses Dynamic Soaring to fly the oceans without ever needing land. They only come back to mate.

For humans, Dynamic Soaring is a combination of skills that leads to personal change mastery. These skills include:

- **Discernment:** Noticing and correctly interpreting signs from our bodies, minds, and environment allows us to see opportunities, manage responses, and reach soaring gracefully earlier in our journey.

- **Motivation:** Staying focused on the rewards of the journey and celebrating every time we step forward in skill, belief, or resource levels.

- **Perspective:** Staying high, where the path is easier, diving down to see more clearly when we need to, and gliding through. This will decrease the overall effort and fuel required for our journey.

- **Vulnerability:** Our willingness to be our whole selves. When we accept who we are, and allow others to see our journey, we can be an inspiration to others. This can provide fuel for our journey too.

- **Commitment:** Our unrelenting focus on journey's end. We stay flexible on the how and watch for opportunities to celebrate each day.

Suddenly Graceful

By the end of the season, Alex leaves the little island, traveling thousands of leagues, soaring gracefully, and reveling in the joy of flight. It is all worth it.

Wow! Our Change Journey seems to be over quite suddenly. A feeling of ease has been growing for some time now. We have a growing confidence, and have started to share our learning with others. We are even having fun.

What now?

Enjoy it. It's time to revel in our new mastery. Take the time to rest, relax, and recuperate fully.

Take a life survey. What other changes may have stalled in your life? The more we can bring all the smaller changes into completion, the more content and fulfilled we experience our life to be day to day.

Over time, we catch clues earlier and discern that it is time to change again. The earlier we catch it, the less drastic it needs to be. It becomes another opportunity to shape the chaos and put our change skills to use.

Enjoy the journey.

Remember to send us a postcard!

Part Three: Master Change

Ready to smooth out the edges, shorten the trip, and migrate confidently through your change? Read on! This part has the "how to" that makes all the difference.

Welcome to the Club!

Change is happening in every part of our lives. For some we are in the Normal phase, and for others the Resistance Pattern has been running for days, weeks, or years. Likely, in one area of life, things still feel new and awkward, not yet slipstream. For each change in our world, we are navigating the same Change Journey.

The overlapping journeys of change can leave us disoriented and bereft of hope that we will ever "arrive." Some find comfort in embracing the idea that there is no destination. Their focus on a never-ending journey is a work-around for the frustration and disappointment that comes from being lost on the seas for so long.

We take umbrage with the "change never ends" theory for two reasons.

1. The chaos created by having multiple Change Journeys open at once leaves a trail of confusion. It is a game of Pin the Tail on the Donkey to find the best response for our feelings, odd behaviours, or resistance in each moment.

2. Completing a Change Journey creates competence, confidence, and releases energy back into our lives—all things that you deserve to celebrate.

We maintain that when you know how to read and respond to the signs of change, you can make an informed choice about the micro adjustments required to maintain your momentum toward Soaring Gracefully.

On the Same Page

Let's start this deep dive by making sure we are all on the same page. We know we are using some terms you may or may not know from other areas of your life. Take the time to consider each one. As you do, the tools will seem to be more accessible and have greater impact.

Change Journey

The Change Journey is how we, as humans, respond to the desire to move into greater authenticity. We step through life as old patterns dissolve into chaos and reform into a more efficient and brilliant order that feels closer and closer to home. Our levels of personal mastery determine whether we view our role in this change as victim or author.

Once change begins, we move through a resistance pattern, then ideally on to the growth pattern. How long we spend in each one will depend on our awareness and willingness to engage with the Change Journey. Added to that is our level of willingness to detach from the old and embrace more of our true self.

Common changes already have a game plan we can borrow from others—moving, changing jobs, or starting a family are all big changes. There are so many people willing to help us out.

Our own personal evolution is a change that is slower and much harder to recognize. When our Model of the World expands but our environment does not, then we feel crunchy and start pecking at our shell. It sneaks up on us.

Often an outside perspective is needed to see how we are shaping our new future.

Landmarks

Landmarks are the big turning points along the Change Journey. There is either a growing or easing of tensions in relation to these landmarks and this provides context for our experience. The landmarks you see on the image of the Change Journey are:

A. **Normal:** Normal is a time in our world where there are few surprises. Whether we are pleased or frustrated by our circumstances isn't relevant, we always know what to expect and how to successfully problem-solve.

B. **Moment of Change:** This is the moment the old pattern dissolves. Whether we perceive the change as by choice or by circumstance, it often has a feeling of suddenness about it.

C. **The Decision:** This is a moment of clarity created by drawing a line in the sand. We decide that moving forward into the development of the new pattern is preferable to the discomfort caused by our attachment to the old.

D. **Soaring Gracefully:** As we enter the realm of mastery, there is an ease and flow to this new pattern that we can discern and guide. The whole journey comes into view and we can appreciate the value of each failed takeoff and bit of turbulence along the way.

Crosswinds

Crosswinds are signals to adjust our flight pattern. Our level of personal mastery determines how powerful the crosswinds need to be to gain our attention to course-correct. The best response to a crosswind depends on which landmark we are approaching or have just passed.

Updrafts

An updraft is that experience of everything moving into flow with increasing momentum. The more updraft, the more we know we are "on course" in the Change Journey. Updraft comes to mean that we are in the right place at the right time and can focus in on the learning that is presenting itself—even if we don't yet see how it matters to the whole.

Resistance

The variations on resistance are vast. Suffice it to say, you experience resistance when you are attached. We often start by being attached to the old pattern, or how we choose to control the current chaos that has enveloped our lives. Later, we find that we become attached to the outcome and attempt to force the change to meet the image we created. Regardless, resistance has a low-frequency feel to it and our emotions can range from despondent, to frustrated, to defiant.

Surrender

Surrender has long been a topic of discussion. It has several meanings depending on the context. In our world, surrendering is less about giving up and more about leaning in. The degree of trust we have in ourselves is the sole indicator of our ability to surrender through leaning in. When we trust ourselves to bounce, recover, discern, and laugh, leaning in seems the best option. If the word "surrender" still feels unsettling, try "yield" instead. That did the trick for us.

The Change Journey

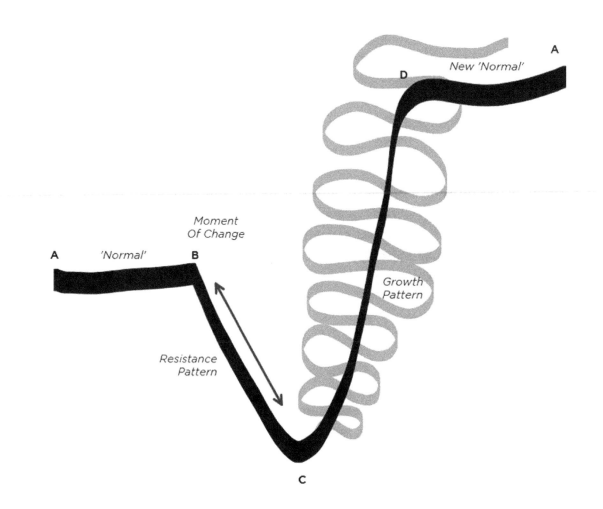

Your Change Journey Experience

The gifts of embarking on the Change Journey are many. You uncover more of your true authentic self, expand your Model of World, meet amazing new people, and create a confidence loop that grows every time you experience yourself moving from awkward to mastery in your new patterns. How cool is that?

First, we need to dissect the Change Journey so you can recognize and orient yourself from within.

Let's lay this out like you are a fictional uber master in life. An uber master, like Alex, who chooses to only do one change at a time. A human of such advanced character and personal mastery that your skills of discernment are legendary. Studied by all the serious personal-development gurus across the globe.

Then, we will weave in how we actually manage our day-to-day juggle of the differing change journeys while attempting to discern the difference between a "sign" that needs a response and an upset tummy from adventures of week-old leftovers we had for supper last night.

Normal

From the moment the last change completes and next change begins, we call the time of "Normal." At the start of "Normal" stress is low, and you enjoy a sense of accomplishment and pride. For some big changes, this may be the state for the rest of your life. For others it may be a temporary time of rest before you take flight again. For Alex, he was rocking his egg.

When the current pattern is set for another upgrade, small tensions start to weave themselves into your world. They show up at first as irritations, then frustrations, and finally an impassioned plea for something more amazing in your world.

When you become aware of either your frustrations, or strange new opportunities that keep popping up, then you can settle into the idea that change is coming and plan your takeoff.

If you become attached to the idea that there is safety in the familiar, resistance to start your change begins to build. As the resistance builds, the degree of pressure required to release the pattern grows. The signs of this upcoming change become louder and more insistent. It takes the dedication of an ostrich to still be totally surprised when it happens.

The other choice is to channel your inner Alex and get to pecking on the shell—only Alex has control over the hatching.

Resistance Pattern

Change is disruptive. Whether you embrace the change in awareness, or it seems like the world pulls the rug out from under you, things are in a bit of a shambles—bits of eggshell scattered everywhere.

What happens next is entirely dependent on how aware you are of the change and its implications for your life.

Without knowledge and awareness, the first reaction is panic, and the focus is on getting back to normal (which is no longer possible). There is a scrambling on the slippery slope. Every tool and skill that used to work so well during the "Normal" times is tried again and again with the hope that all the pieces can be reformed.

Depending on the person, this backward striving and yearning for the good ol' times can lead to a victimhood mentality filled with anger and brooding. This is the way of the dodo bird.

Even the best of us spends some time in this place—no one likes having their sandcastles kicked over. We say, "Have a good stomp around—pout like you mean it!" Then get on with it. We can promise you that life will get louder and louder until you do.

When you are aware of the change, you can have your little pout and then move to put out the fires. Then check on your commitments. Do any of them need to be renegotiated? What support systems do you need to activate to ensure you continue to get your physical, emotional, mental, and spiritual needs met? Who is stable in your world who can be there for you?

Next, there is loss to deal with. Grieving is an important process. Even when you choose change, the loss of the comfortable, normal, or even the irritations you became used to have all left impressions in your world that need to be released. Take the time to find the lessons you want to keep and make a list of what you want to be different in your future.

Once you become complete with the past, you will naturally find attention moving to the future. You will acknowledge your own right to grow and find you are curious about what is to become.

The moment you complete the Resistance Pattern will be marked in time. There is a definite change in focus and a release of the past. How hard you have fought or embraced the change will determine whether landmark **C** is marked with a loud declaration followed by fireworks or a calm and poignant moment of silence that rings through the night. Alex decided he wanted the skies more than anything.

Growth Pattern

There is a lot to do here. The list includes weaving your new resources, new skills, and updated Model of the World to finally claim ownership over your new pattern.

Like Alex wearing a path in the sand and learning to thrive in the skies, this pattern takes the longest in time. With a greater revelation of your true self, you are capable of so much more. The issue is that you are still in the habit of being the older version of you. So, it is time for as much patience, perseverance, and celebration as you can muster.

albatross as an example of how to travel along this part of your journey. ...n be super awkward getting off the beach, once in the air, there is so much ... in store for you too.

Resources

What got you here won't get you there. This adage is very appropriate. As "obstacles" seem to form in front of you on this portion of the journey, it will feel like they have taken you off course. In truth, they are leading you to the resources you need, like additional funds, specific learning, new opportunities, and other tools to assist you.

Watch for new people further ahead on the journey. Know that your relationships with others will change over time. Some will take on a smaller role in your world while others become the stars of the show.

Embrace the perspective that everything can be woven in to propel you forward. Find the gaps and fill them with amazing people and skills so that you will become the person who can easily hold this change.

Skills

Even superpowers need time to be harnessed and put to good use. The trick is to stay focused through the awkward stage as you grow in competence. Then you will naturally start to teach others coming up behind you. Your willingness to put in the time to practise will keep you moving forward.

Be aware that sometimes skills you learn are part of a larger skill package you are building. So, stay focused even if it seems small.

Model of the World 2.0

The thing that Karen and I love the most is the feeling you get when your Model of the World gets an upgrade. Your new perspective changes the meaning that you place on everything in your world. As old beliefs struggle to keep up and peel away, a more expanded world view is revealed that applies more broadly. You can also tell you have elevated your beliefs when you feel less "judgy" toward yourself and others.

Imagine how much more Alex can see from the skies!

Claim It

Even as this growth pattern continues to take up more energy, personal management, and focus than you would like it to, you soon begin to find the rhythm taking shape in your world. As you keep to this beat, your intuition grows along with your discernment and the fun factor grows.

As you cross the halfway point, you start to feel the momentum increase. Things are easier and you find yourself laughing.

All the twists and turns of your journey come rushing back and you start to connect the dots. What seemed so off track, now you see as totally on point. The view is amazing from here!

This is the time that all your effort is paying off and you feel you have earned the right to settle back into a new "normal" that you would never trade for the old.

You are Here: Finding Yourself in the Change Journey

After this overview, you might be super curious about where you are in your own change journey. Well, we have an assessment for that!

You can find the link at www.alexthealbatross.com.

Recognizing Crosswinds and How to Course-Correct

Crosswinds are signals to adjust our flight pattern. Our level of personal mastery determines how powerful the crosswinds need to be to gain our attention to course-correct. An updraft is that experience of everything moving into flow with increasing momentum. The more updraft, the more we know we are "on course" in the Change Journey.

There are three ways to turn a crosswind into an updraft that we want you to discover and start using right away.

Crosswind		Updraft
Isolation	➤	Resourcing
Presuming	➤	Discernment
Attachment	➤	Neutrality

Success Tips

- Do each exercise. This will create familiarity and you will know which exercise you need in the future.

- When asked, use specific memories. Generalities create muted responses and do not have nearly enough data.

- Download the worksheets and access video tutorials at www.alexthealbatross. com.

- Be gentle with yourself and give yourself permission to take your time.

Exercise 1: Moving from Isolation to Resourcing (Team Awesome)

Were you praised, as a child, every time you did something all by yourself? As a stage of development, being self-sufficient is an important element of maturity. When "not needing any help" is presented as the goal, we can miss out on the opportunities to learn how to grow faster and have fun as we grow with others. Learning how to work with others in a way that lifts everyone up is a skill set, and now is a great time to further develop it in the name of gracefully soaring.

Isolation is believing that you are all on your own, and that you need to do it by yourself. You try to solve all the problems and find all the solutions yourself. You may be worried about looking foolish or getting in over your head. Your focus becomes presenting the best image of success and stability even when everything really feels like a hot mess.

Isolation is a major cause of crosswinds on your Change Journey. Isolation deprives us of a wide variety of perspectives, ideas, assistance, and most importantly momentum. When faced with new experiences, and the common misdiagnoses of your body's data, it is easy to feel overwhelmed. Buffeted by the challenges of the Change Journey, you may want to just hide and hope it all blows over.

Resourcing is reaching out, tapping in, and being open to assistance. It builds something more than you could do alone—more than the sum of the parts. Talking a challenge out with a friend, partnering with a colleague, and asking a mentor are all resourcing. First and foremost, you start with yourself. Internal resourcing is about your connection with your own intuition and mental acuity—you are your first resource.

External resourcing requires vulnerability, a willingness to be our whole selves. When we accept who we are, and allow others to see our journey, we are more willing to reach out, to ask for help. In turn, this can be an inspiration to others and provide fuel for our journey.

How to Move from Isolation to Resourcing

To transform the crosswind of isolation into an updraft, resourcing is required. It's easy to get in your own way and stay in isolation, especially when you tell yourself stories about what it means to ask for assistance.

This activity will highlight the mental blocks that influence the tendency to isolate at the time we need to resource the most. You may find that you have lots of people, few, or even no one. Take heart, we will chat at the end about how to surround yourself with the amazing people you can journey with.

Review each situation and write in your go-to resourcing person/people. If you haven't resourced in the situation before, consider who you might reach out to if you did.

1. **"I don't want to bother anyone."**

It's common for independent people to not want to be a bother or take up someone else's time. People love to be asked for advice, to brainstorm, or to offer support. Just like you!

Who always has your back and will offer a sounding board or suggestions?

_____

2. **"I don't want to look foolish."**

When a smart, successful person hits a problem, they may avoid resourcing. You want to be seen like you have it all together, so asking for help feels like getting naked in the park.

Who will honour your growth and assist in finding solutions?

_____

3. **"They are trying to solve my problem."**

You may have had people in the past attempt to solve your problem for you. Before you ask for it, they give advice, solutions, recommendations. Or they decide that the problem is you and offer unsolicited coaching.

Who will hold space for you with curiosity and support so you can solve the problem?

_____

4. **"They are ignoring my problem."**

It's frustrating to go to a person who tells you that you are awesome, wonderful, and amazing and tries to convince you that you don't really have a problem.

Who will really listen and ask the questions because you are awesome?

_____

5. **"I'm fine."/"I'm doing okay."**

When you are in the change process you may feel like you are doing okay. You may be unaware that you are missing something, or don't know what questions to ask. If this is you AND you are not moving as quickly or easily as you'd like, it's time to resource.

Who will be curious and ask you questions to tease out the blocks?

_____

6. **Who comes to you?**

Consider who comes to you when they need help with any of these things and check in to see if they are on your lists. They might be or they might not be.

_____

Applying Resourcing in Real Time

Your list may look like the who's who, or you may have one or two people that show up again and again. You might have few people or no one on your lists. Here is what to do next.

Feeling good about your list of people? Keep those relationships fresh and consider sending out your gratitude. Let them know how important they are to you.

Realize you have a few gaps? Cultivate a team of amazing people around you who will hold space for you, poke at your stuff, ask the tough questions, and brainstorm solutions.

List a little bare? This can really sneak up on you. We recommend that you have a look at the people who demonstrate good resourcing. You see them asking for a shoulder and offering to assist too. Sometimes the best place to start is with a pro, and be very literal when you ask them to mentor you.

The more resourceful you are willing to be, the faster crosswinds become updrafts. You find that you are tapped into yourself and calling yourself on all your sh . . . stuff. Then your discernment about what you need from others and what you can offer them becomes clear. Ask any bird; it's fun to fly together.

Additional resources, like our Top Five mini training, are waiting for you at www.alexthealbatross.com.Building and leveraging a great flock around you is within your reach.

Exercise 2: Moving from Presumption to Discernment (Map Me)

Ready to find out if your Model of the World is telling it to you straight?

So much information is streaming in through your experience moment to moment. As it does, you match it to the inner maps of your Model of the World so that you know how you "normally" respond. If your maps are outdated or mislabeled, then your response is also outdated or mismatched. This creates confusion when things go differently than you expected and decays trust in yourself.

During change, two things are key to staying on course—accurate maps and the discernment to know which of your many maps to use. A focus on three of these maps will make the most difference in creating a smoother and shorter change journey.

This exercise has been designed for you to check and update these three maps for accuracy while building your discernment. This way, when you need them most, you can be confident that you will know which map to use and that it will point you in the right direction.

Intuition of Warning Map: Your amazing self sifts and sorts all the incoming data based on what is most deeply important to you. When actions are contrary to the best interests you have set for yourself, then your intuition responds with a strong sensation to warn you.

Adrenaline Response Map: Your body physically prepares for you to take immediate action and the sensations in the body are predictable.

Mental Response Map: Your mind is so good at running resistance patterns *monkey mind* and the physical sensations are different and identifiable.

What map gets you into the most trouble?

How to Move from Presumption to Discernment

We are going to do this in three steps. You have permission to just do one, none, or all three.

1. First, let's start with collecting some specific memories of experiences and how you mapped them in the past.

2. Then, some information about how your body responds automatically in those circumstances—regardless of how you mapped them.

3. Finally, you will assess what your own responses "mean" to you now in your Model of the World and decide what your response will be in future.

By the end, you will build deeper trust in yourself. With the trust, your ability to discern the need for navigational tweaks will grow and you will dynamically soar through your change journey.

Step One: Collect Memories

It is time to take a dance through your past. Choose intense experiences so that you can recall the physical responses to record. The good news is that intense experiences are encoded more specifically and more intensely in our memories, making them easier to recall and even re-experience at varying degrees.

As you complete this exercise, remember that specific moments will hold more data than any collection of experiences. So be specific. If you trip into a memory that is unpleasant in some way because of how you understood it or the aftermath, remember this truth—you have already lived through it and have incorporated learning and wisdom from it.

You can choose to write directly in the book or download worksheets and watch tutorials from www.alexthealbatross.com.

A. **Intuition of Warning Map:** When actions are contrary to the best interests you have set for yourself, then your intuition responds with a strong sensation to warn you. Often, you need to backtrack to find the moment your gut told you "Heck no!" These memories often start during the regret portion of the experience when you are realizing that you "knew" right at the beginning. So, let's start there.

Example: Laying on the couch with my arm flung out, vaguely pointing the remote at the TV I couldn't even see, as the tears streamed down into my ears, I was feeling the disappointment and betrayal of being let down by a person I trusted. While flipping channels like an automaton I suddenly shot right up as a memory raced from across time and showed me the moment my body shouted its warning at me—move on from this person. It started like a deep tremor in my gut and moved up through my chest.

MEMORY OF REGRET	MOMENT OF INTUITION	SENSATION
Laying on the couch feeling sorry for myself	*The moment before I decided to trust anyway*	*Deep tremor in my gut that moved up through my chest*

B. **Adrenaline Response Map**: When your brain doesn't recognize a situation, or believes it to be dangerous, it automatically prepares for every contingency—fight/flight/faint/freeze. It expects that you will need to respond physically in some way. Adrenaline is the tool of choice. As it courses through your body, your heart rate raises and the blood drains from the parts of your brain you use for complex thought—it's all about right here, right now. So, what memories do you have of when your body prepared to act on your behalf?

Example: I stood on stage, half in front of the podium. The slide projecting on the mammoth screen was vaguely familiar. I looked out on a sea of people. All I could hear was my heart pounding in my ears. I felt removed from my body. I felt my vocal cords begin to move as I read the first part of my notes aloud. In a few minutes, I felt back in control and hoped the words I had spoken at the beginning didn't give me away.

MEMORY OF READY TO ACT	SENSATION
First time on a stage in front of two hundred people	*Pounding heart, "out of body" feeling, slow thinking, faint feeling*

C.   **Mental Response Map:** Resistance patterns that are constructed by the mind can show up in a myriad of ways. Your mind will have your favourites. To find these past experiences, start with times you were stalled by your thoughts, your mind was spinning, or you were caught up in the monkey mind.

Example: Sitting and staring at the contracts, I was weighing all the pros and cons. They whirled around in my head like frenzied sparrows. I couldn't find the important points, the points that would give me clarity. As I look back, I don't know if I was even in my body. I was so committed to just figuring this out—trying to divine the future and know the right path forward. It still makes me nauseous to remember it.

MEMORY	THOUGHTS	SENSATION
Decision to sign those contracts	*"What if"s, pros and cons, worries about the money*	*Nausea, disassociation, tight shoulders*

Step Two: Checking Your Map Accuracy

Diving a little deeper into how your body is physically responding will bring greater discernment to the sensations and how to recognize them in the future—even when things are feeling hairy.

1. **Intuition** is that internal nudge to lean in or stay away.

   There is building research into the gut-brain axis, known as the "second brain." This second brain is considered important in intuitive reasoning and what we call "gut feelings." There is so much experience being collected and processed out of our awareness in the gut-brain axis. To tap in and interpret the data from our gut intuition requires discernment.

   For those of us who lean more on our minds and like to *know*, we often discount our intuition if we can't explain where it came from. Karen and I only regret the times we discounted our gut.

   Mapping it is vital for you to build greater trust in yourself. Trust that you will always know what you need and when you need it.

2. The **Adrenal Response** is the complex physiological response to the possibility of action.

   Our bodies are so amazing. They have been finely tuned for survival since we lived on the grasslands and in caves. When our environment was filled with dangers, it was especially useful to have an internal mechanism that had us ready in an instant to fight or flee as appropriate.

   Today, sadly, we are short on sabre-toothed tigers to use as an excuse. Most of the time, we have simply imagined something new and our body responds and floods our system with adrenaline. The idea of stepping onto a stage, or applying for a new position, or asking that amazing person out has our adrenaline coursing through us.

This response in your body can be confused with your gut intuition if you have yet to build the discernment. Imagine feeling the rush of adrenaline at the thought of true love and not actioning because you misdiagnose it as your gut telling you that person is bad news. Or, even more common, passing off your screaming intuition to run for simple nervousness.

3. The **Mental Response** is our mind's reaction and ongoing assessment of a situation.

   With over 12,000 thoughts per day, of which 95% are repetitive, you can imagine how equipped we are to assess any change in our world. The National Science Foundation, out of Virginia, estimates that 80% of our thoughts are negative.

   With this data, start to take your initial "thoughts" with a grain of salt. When things are new, you may need to learn new ways of thinking about your new context—this is building your Mental Acuity.

   As a crosswind, our thoughts can take over. They get loud, race in your brain, and drown out the other data your body has to offer. Your mind racing has a sensation that is different from your gut and your adrenaline response when you are "ready to act."

Step Three: Your Analysis

Now it is time to reflect.

Go back through each of the memories you recorded and ask yourself the following list of questions. Use these questions to assess how your map was labeled then, how it is labeled now, and what changes you would like to make. You will find that reading this book has updated some of the maps already.

Questions for Reflection—ask them for each memory you recorded

1. How did you explain your reaction in that moment? What did you think was going on inside of you?

2. Were there any other explanations in the mix? From a friend or even your own mind?

3. Looking back with all your experience, wisdom, and learning, how do you explain it now?

4. If you were faced with a similar situation tomorrow, what would be your first clue that this was the map you were working with?

5. How would you prefer to respond?

After your contemplation, it is time to record your findings. Now that you know where you were presuming and can build further discernment, you and your body can be working in concert toward your amazing outcomes.

We have provided a worksheet here for each of the areas:

1. Intuition of Warning

2. Adrenal Response

3. Mental Response

You can also download a one-page map with all three areas to complete and post up where you know you will see it. Find it at www.alexthealbatross.com. Then take a picture and post it with the hashtag #MapMeAlex.

Intuition of Warning Map:

SENSATION	HOW I USED TO REACT	HOW I CHOOSE TO RESPOND
Deep tremor in my gut that moved up through my chest	Let my mind tell me I was just making things up	Take a time out to listen to myself and then trust in it

Adrenaline Response Map:

SENSATION	HOW I USED TO REACT	HOW I CHOOSE TO RESPOND
Pounding heart, "out of body" feeling, slow thinking, faint feeling	Back out or procrastinate	Take slow breaths and find one small thing that will take me forward

Mental Response Map:

SENSATION	HOW I USED REACT	HOW I CHOOSE TO RESPOND
Nausea, disassociation, tight shoulders	*Follow my thoughts around hoping they make sense*	*Stop. Take a breath. Observe the situation. Proceed.*

Applying Discernment in Real Time

Completing this exercise creates an increase in awareness. The next time you experience any of these sensations, it will allow you to step back and assess all the incoming data. You will find that you are more confident about making decisions in changing conditions and you will build a lifelong trust with yourself that will continue to serve you.

Keep your assessment close as you continue to build discernment and remap what the data *means* to you over time.

Exercise 3: Moving from Attachment to Neutrality (Wooden Box)

Resistance is the result of attachment. One of the biggest crosswinds that can buffet anyone on the Change Journey until they are battered and worn is resistance. The trick is to have a way to release attachment as soon as you become aware of it. This is the top exercise that will move you into an updraft that will smooth out the turbulence and speed up your journey.

Let's start with defining "attachment" and "neutrality," and then dive into the exercise.

Attachment

A monkey trap. This is the most apt description of how attachment creates crosswinds while we are on the Change Journey. Let us explain. A monkey trap consists of a secured container sporting a hole just large enough for a monkey to slip their open hand through. Inside is the bait—something the monkey doesn't think they can live without—a banana or favourite nut. When the monkey puts their hand in and closes it around the bait, the fist they create is now too big to fit back through the hole. The only way to get their hand back out is to release what they are holding. The trap is voluntary.

Every time we try to hold onto "how things used to be," or force an outcome in our world, we are behaving like we are in a monkey trap. Letting go is a release that opens opportunities to find more bananas elsewhere. It is a choice we can make at any moment—assuming we are even aware it is happening.

The other feature of note that comes with attachment is that it feels heavy. Tiny threads of attachment to things, preferences, what you need to be right about, and your hopes, plans, and certainties about the future. It is a lot to track and takes energy to maintain.

Neutrality

Very separate from how much you *care*, neutrality is the result of focus.

Focus is the narrowing of perspective and release of everything that has come before or is yet to be. This simplifies everything. No racing minds. No overwhelm. No old stories. Just you and the possibilities alive in this very moment.

In your Change Journey, neutrality allows you to live more authentically and aligned to your true self. We do this by maintaining focus on the present.

Mastering the state of neutrality opens an experience of expanded time and awareness. Your sensitivity rises and assists your discernment. You can assess all the data and be content to wait until you are complete to make your choices. The deepening sense of being attuned to yourself builds trust and confidence in your own abilities over time. Flowing from this is a sense of curiosity about each outcome and how the experience will move you closer.

How to Move from Attachment to Neutrality

Training your focus on the present is a skill set and this activity is intended to build that skill. The more time you spend focused in the present, the more you feel at home and wonder how you ever managed to get anything done before this.

100% Present Activity (Wooden Box Exercise)

The busyness of the brain, scattered focus, and attachment cause us to live in the past or the future. We spend all kinds of energy on reliving old stories or making up possible new ones. Whether we are busy with crappy or fun thoughts, we end up feeling pulled in all directions. Getting 100% present allows for a richer experience in our now, filled with authenticity, creativity, and curiosity.

This is a quiet exercise to go inside and become 100% present, curious, and ready to receive guidance and wisdom from yourself. It is not a time for personal therapy or "working through" anything. We just want a place to put all the circling thoughts and cares for later.

To deepen the experience of this exercise, read through the instructions first. Some find it helpful to record the instructions so they can sit back and close their eyes. We have a recording to guide you through this exercise at www.alexthealbatross.com and a pretty download too.

The Wooden Box Exercise

This exercise will take three to eight minutes. Through this exercise you may become aware of something new. You may see it, hear it, feel it, know it—however you receive it is perfect.

- Find a quiet space, and sitting or lying down, get comfortable.
- Gently, allow your eyes to close.
- Take a few relaxing breaths.
- Imagine a large wooden box with its lid wide open.
- As you breathe in and out, see all the things you are reliving from the past or imagining for the future swirling around you—people, responsibilities, memories, worries, hopes (all the things that are taking up space in your thoughts right now).
- Gently and with love, guide each item (including all the sensations associated with it) into the wooden box.
- Know that these things are in the wooden box for safekeeping. You can take them back out any time or you may choose to leave some there indefinitely.
- Once everything has been guided into the box with love, close the lid.
- With the past and future concerns safely tucked away, let's choose a new focus.
- Take a deep breath in . . . and out.

- Focus into your body in the now. Place your full attention right behind your belly button—this is your sacred centre.
- Notice the sensations in your body:
    - Notice the breath in your chest.

    - Notice your fingers.

    - Notice the fabric on your back.

    - Notice the sensation of your hair on your head.

    - Notice the tiny muscles in your eyelids.

- As you continue to notice your body in the now, be curious.
- Ask yourself: "What am I ignoring right now that I need to be aware of?"
- Breathe gently, allowing yourself to see/hear/feel and know the answers. (Take all the time you need.)
- With loving kindness, thank yourself for this time and this knowledge, for the love and space you are giving to yourself.
- When you are ready, gently open your eyes.

Using a single question is most effective. The single focus, maintained over minutes, allows for deeper answers to rise to your conscious awareness. You may choose to repeat the question a few times, honouring your own process.

The next time you do the exercise, you may consider one of these questions instead:

- What is possible in this moment?
- What do I most need right now?

Applying Neutrality in Real Time

Even in the most stressful of times, your focus in the present will serve you. You will find that time feels like it is unrolling more slowly, and the present expands out around you. There will be time. You will notice so much more in each moment. Your decisions and actions will serve you both in that moment and throughout your Change Journey.

Over time, you will get so good at putting everything you don't need in this moment into the box. This insistence on focus over distraction will loosen attachments and you will begin to see choices you never noticed before—what fun!

Part Four: Conclusion

Weaving the Wisdom

In truth, changes come in all sizes and in all parts of your life. Most people have Change Journeys open in more than one area of life and are at varying degrees of resistance or embrace with each of them. To make sense of it all will take some introspection on your part.

Here are our top ten tips for increasing the amount of graceful soaring in your world.

1. **Map every Change Journey** that is open and not yet complete in your world. Start with a life wheel and map every Change Journey, small and large, you can find in your world. Then take a step back and say, "Wow! With all that going on I still manage to get dressed most days—I deserve a high-five!"

2. **Choose a practice change.** One where you can see the whole journey even though it is not yet complete. Orient yourself on the journey and use this book as a resource as you complete that journey.

3. **Focus on changes** that are smaller at first. The more you can complete, the more your resources are freed up for the ones that seem bigger.

4. **Track and celebrate every accomplishment.** It can be easy to underestimate how amazing your accomplishments are as you go day to day comparing your blooper reel with another person's sizzle reel. Stay focused on your own progress—that is where your self-satisfaction lives.

5. **Decide to embrace the belief** that you are everything that you need to be. That Change Journeys are intended to be stair steps to the big reveal of the true self we already are underneath. Feel a thrill every time the opportunity for another peak arises.

6. **Master these tools** and then come and get some more. There is so much we can share with you. Let's start here and show you how effective you can be in your day-to-day world. Then we can talk about weaving in some more fun things along the way.

7. **Join the flock.** After reading and applying this book, you will likely want to find more people who qualify as your "birds of a feather." Gather to share stories, insights, and lessons learned. (V-shaped formation optional.)

8. **Stop pretending** that you know what is happening. You are in the throes of change. Just be open and curious to what it all means.

9. **Giggle** . . . often. If you are going to journey anyway, you might as well be having fun.

10. **Share your Journey** with others. Be willing to inspire others so that everything you are going through has value for you AND others. It can really make it all worth it.

To your magnificence,
Karen and Karen

Alex's Next Adventure

It's been eleven years since Alex launched into the skies to fly across the ocean. In that time, Alex has become so proficient in gliding that hours often pass without the flap of a wing. A practiced eye finds fish from high above.

Over the past few months, something has been pulling. A sensation deep inside that has Alex returning to the island where it all started. Not knowing what to expect, but trusting deeply, Alex navigates confidently into the night.

As the island comes into view, Alex notices the bustle of many, many albatross.

Alex is checking out the area when one albatross stands out in the most amazing way. The landing is not graceful, but now, back on earth, Alex feels like dancing.

Starting with a quick bow, both albatross begin to posture, 3.5 metre (11 foot) wingspan stretched wide and head stretched forth. Bills glide and tap like a fencing match. The clicking and vocalizing is elaborate as they dance in a mesmerizing and intricate mating ritual.

This is the day that Alex's life changes again.

What an amazing journey awaits!

Thank you!

No one travels alone—at least not further than the grocery store.

List of Our Peeps

Here are the amazing people who we have traveled with us in the birthing of this book (so far).

A special thanks to our closest peeps and biggest supporters:

Kevin Rost and Jeff Kessler

Dave and Bonnie Collacutt, and Alf and Carol Whittaker

Jackie Stickwood and Adwynna MacKenzie

Laura Zeidler, Shannon Zangari, Debbie Young, Gillian Joy Wyatt, Ravella Wiles, Carol Whittaker, Alf Whittaker, Carol Ward, Denise Tucker, Neli Trevisan, Richard Tremblay, Jennifer Trask, Dionne Thompson, Mikalya Thatcher, Ron Stevens, Brenda St. Amand, Patti Smith, Joanna Shaw, Roberta Robbins, Lisa Reaume, Kristen Rayner, Leanne Quesnelle, Keli-Ann Pye-Beshara, Jill Proud, Jamie Ollivier, Katherine Nelson-Riley, DJ Moye, Laura Morrison, Jessy Morrison, Angela Martin-King, Nanci MacDonald, Vanessa Long, Nikki Lee, Alyssa Labrecque, Fran Kruse, Sarah Khaki, Briar Kelly, Erin Johnson, Ladanna James, David Hyde, Kate Howes, Karen Hicks, Judy Harrigan, Joyce Groskopf, Joy Goch, Nikki Glahn, Jackie Galvin, Kerri Fullerton, Laura Freeman, Ashley Fortier, Cathy Doyle, Dr. Martine Divera, Patricia Dent, Trisha Cuthbertson, Paula Crane, Amy Courser, Dave Collacutt, Bonnie Collacutt, Heather Chernofshy, Daniella Chase, Bradley Charbonneau, Sue Carr, Judith Cane, Cynthia Breadner, Jessie Brandon, Gina Bello, Kimberly Banfield, Jonathan Audette, Jamie Armstrong, Thomas Ambeau.

A special shout out to Bruce Peters for the amazing cover design!

About the Authors

Karen Collacutt

Karen Collacutt Makes it Go! She loves the thrill of the journey and feels deeply into every curve of her dynamic soaring. Sometimes she forgets that she is human and takes responsibility for the entire world—and she rocks it! Karen has a lot of love to spare and spreads it lavishly on her hubby, pups, family, friends, and the Earth. We love her right back!

Karen Kessler

Karen Kessler is the Universal Translator, mashing all kinds of learning into cool new thoughts. She makes magic with words from her mind, heart, and funny bone. She sees the flow of things, adjusting her wings to balance the crosswinds and make the most of the updrafts. Karen snuggles puppies, kitties, and her honey. She is quick to giggle, opens her heart wide, and loves big. She rocks!

Endnotes

[i] Lanting, Frans. "'Learning to Fly' Frans Lanting and the Young Albatrosses of Midway." YouTube. Uploaded by Chris Eckstrom, September 7, 2010, www.youtube.com/watch?v=2H9PQ6jt9us.

[ii] DeMichele, Thomas. "An Albatross Can Fly Around the World Without Landing." Fact/Myth, www.factmyth.com/factoids/an-albatross-can-fly-around-the-world-without-landing/.

[iii] A Life Wheel shows the key areas of life that we value. We have one at www.alexthealbatross.com you are welcome to download and use for this work.

Your Notes

CPSIA information can be obtained
at www.ICGtesting.com
Printed in the USA
BVHW050723261121
621896BV00003B/5